It's Tot Shabbat!

Naomi Danis

photographs by Tod Cohen

KAR-BEN
PUBLISHING

In honor of my mother, Ruth Stern Danis and in memory of my
father Seymour Danis, z"l, and for Sophie, Ezra and Talya Danis
Oberfield, and all the children of the Forest Hills Jewish Center,
young and old, with love

—N.D.

In loving memory of Stanley Cohen

—T.C.

Kar-Ben Publishing
A division of Lerner Publishing Group, Inc.
241 First Avenue North
Minneapolis, MN 55401 U.S.A.
1-800-4-KARBEN

Website address: www.karben.com

Library of Congress Cataloging-in-Publication Data

Danis, Naomi.
    It's tot Shabbat! / by Naomi Danis ; photographs by Tod Cohen.
        p.   cm.
    ISBN: 978-0-7613-4515-2 (lib. bdg. : alk. paper)
    1. Sabbath—Juvenile literature. 2. Preschool children. I. Cohen, Tod. II. Title.
BM685.D295 2011
296.4'1—dc22   2009030918

Manufactured in the United States of America
1 – DP – 12/15/10

At our synagogue . . .

. . . while the grown-ups pray,
in another room the children play.
This is my Shabbat Club.

Sometimes we say "hello" or "good morning."
Sometimes we feel shy.
Sometimes we feel friendly.

We do puzzles or build with blocks.
We play with dolls and trucks.

We make new friends.

Each week we take out the Torahs.

Everyone gets to hold one.

We listen to a story from the Torah.
Once we read how Noah built an ark.

We pretended to be the animals who came
aboard. We were porcupines!

Another time we read about
the Tower of Babel. The workers didn't
cooperate, and the tower fell down.

Boom!
Our tower fell down, too.
Then we help put away the blocks.

When we can't sit still, it's time to
dance and sing. We hold hands and
go around and around . . .

. . . until we all fall down giggling.

Then we set the table for our Shabbat snack.

"Wait to say the *brachah*," we tell each other.

When everyone has a cup of grape juice and
a piece of challah, we say the blessings.

We say "thank you" for our food and drink.

When we're finished, we go into the sanctuary.

We climb the steps to the *bimah* to sing
"*Adon Olam*" with the whole congregation.

When the prayers are finished, we hug our parents and say "*Shabbat Shalom*" to everyone.

See you again next week!

Blessing Over Wine

בָּרוּךְ אַתָּה יְיָ אֱלֹהֵינוּ מֶלֶךְ הָעוֹלָם בּוֹרֵא פְּרִי הַגָּפֶן.

Baruch Atah Adonai Eloheinu melech ha'olam borei p'ri hagafen.

We praise you, Adonai, who creates the fruit of the vine.

Blessing Over Bread

בָּרוּךְ אַתָּה יְיָ אֱלֹהֵינוּ מֶלֶךְ הָעוֹלָם הַמּוֹצִיא לֶחֶם מִן הָאָרֶץ.

Baruch Atah Adonai Eloheinu melech ha'olam hamotzi lechem min ha'aretz.

We praise you, Adonai, who brings forth bread from the earth.

Glossary

"Adon Olam" – concluding hymn praising God

Brachah – blessing

Challah – Sabbath bread

Shabbat – Jewish Sabbath

Shabbat Shalom – "Have a peaceful Sabbath"

Torah – Scroll of the Five Books of Moses read in the synagogue